DOLLHOUSE FURNISHINGS
for the Bedroom & Bath

Complete Instructions for
Sewing and Making 44 Miniature Projects

Shep Stadtman

DOVER PUBLICATIONS, INC.
New York

Acknowledgments

With love to my husband Jerry for his invaluable encouragement. With sincere appreciation to my family for helping me in so many ways; to my friends Faye Hyman, Joan Melzer, Claire Shostak, Marcia Segal and Hisako Sekijima for their artistic creations, and to my dear grandchildren, Jeffrey Lee Resnik and Olivia Kristina Resnik, for making me see this small dollhouse world through their large eyes.

Dedication

To my daughter Susan F. Resnik,
love and a million thanks for giving me
these exciting creative years,
and for enabling me to meet so many people,
make new friends and fill my time
in a way I never dreamed possible.

Dollhouse Furnishings for the Bedroom and Bath: Complete Instructions for Sewing and Making 44 Miniature Projects is a new work, first published by Dover Publications, Inc., in 1984.

Edited by Laura Marturana.
Book design by Carol Belanger Grafton.
Artwork by Janette Aiello.

Manufactured in the United States of America
Dover Publications, Inc., 31 East 2nd Street, Mineola, N.Y. 11501

Library of Congress Cataloging in Publication Data

Stadtman, Shep.
    Dollhouse furnishings for the bedroom and bath.

    (Dover needlework series)
    1. Doll furniture.   I. Title   II. Series.
TT175.5.S7   1984   745.592′3   83-6222
ISBN 0-486-24590-X (pbk.)

Contents

Introduction

In November of 1976, I received an early morning call from my daughter with a "Mama, help" request. Would I design and sew accessories for her miniature town house? A creative artist, Susan could not sew and was unable to find high quality miniature bed and bath accessories. Bedspreads, curtains, towels and such were generally tossed on a shelf, she explained, or in a basket on the counter for customers to rummage through. They were often wrinkled and soiled from handling. My interest was sparked, so I agreed to give it a try.

The project proved to be delightful and a week later, a "custom boutique" delivery was sent to my daughter. "I love it. Start your own business—it would be terrific," was her reaction, and so I began "Shep's Designery."

My own thoughts about a designer collection were geared toward the discerning collector; I felt that my designs had to be newer and more innovative than anything on the market, and so I made sure that my creations were imaginative, contemporary and available nowhere else on the market. The designs were always attractively boxed or wrapped in plastic, and miniature collectors loved them. I felt quite encouraged when a well-known miniatures shop in New York City placed a substantial order, but when the I. Miller Shoe Salon on Fifth Avenue at 57th Street in New York City displayed my designs in their windows, I knew that "Shep's Designery" was on its way to becoming a mini-household word.

Now, with this book, I would like to offer my collection to the public so that many more miniature houses can be filled with these designs. But this book wouldn't be complete without a word of encouragement to any woman with the dream of having her own business—take the step now! You will never know what you have missed unless you try it.

Miniature Woodworking

Whether you want to duplicate the luxurious room settings shown here, experiment with an original fantasy or reproduce rooms in your own home, you must do first things first—you need the furniture before the quilt, curtains, rugs or any other decorating accessory. You can go out and buy the furniture you will need or you can create your own originals.

This chapter will guide you through working with wood on a small scale so that you can make miniature furniture even if you've never driven a nail, used a saw or sanded a rough edge! In fact, most of the tools in your toolbox will not help you make miniatures—they are too big. One reason that this craft is so popular is because you can make the pieces on your kitchen table using a toothpick and glue instead of a hammer and nails! The following pages combine a general lesson in miniature woodworking with general directions for the pieces in this book. But before you start any project, remember: Read all the directions, organize the steps of your project, gather all your materials and equipment to your working area and measure everything twice!

Equipment

When making miniatures, keep in mind that common household objects can frequently take the place of specific tools. For example, an emery board can sand all but the most detailed softwood shapes, and a single-edged razor blade can saw through many types of wood. You will save time and money by using a Q-tip as a paintbrush, rubber bands as clamps or a toothpick to spread glue.

I have consciously omitted power tools because they are not necessary for the production of many miniatures, including the pieces in this book. However, a power handsaw, such as a jigsaw or saber saw, would save time when cutting the plywood.

CUTTING

X-ACTO Knife: This knife uses different blades to cut various woods and thicknesses. It is probably the most frequently used cutting tool for making miniature furniture.

Scissors: Use sharp household scissors to cut straight and slightly curved balsa-wood shapes. Sharp embroi-

dery scissors are useful for more intricate softwood cuts.

Razor Blades: A single-edged razor blade is useful when straight-cutting balsa and other softwood shapes.

Small Handsaw: Use a coping, tenon or dovetail saw to cut hardwoods, including the basswood and plywood needed for most of the pieces in this book.

Wooden Block: Make all cuts on a wooden block to prevent damage to your work surface.

JOINING

White Glue: Use white glue such as Elmer's® Glue-All™ or Sobo to join wood to wood or wood to fabric. Apply glue sparingly with a toothpick, and wipe away excess glue with a damp cloth.

Small Clamps: Small clamps will help hold pieces together while glue dries or while you are doing additional work that requires two free hands.

Tape: Tape might be the best way to hold small or irregularly shaped pieces together while gluing. Masking tape will work best.

Clothespins: Spring or regular clothespins can be used in place of small clamps.

Rubber Bands: Use rubber bands to hold pieces together in instances where the methods described above might not work, such as for the bed frames in this book.

Epoxy: Use epoxy to join metal to metal or metal to wood. Epoxies are made by mixing two substances together and letting the mixture dry for 5 minutes to 48 hours, depending on the job.

Nails: For miniature woodworking, use the smallest nails you can find, which are also called brads. They are sold in boxes of about 50.

Hammer: Use a small tack or pin hammer to nail components together. Hold the hammer by the end, not the middle, of the handle.

MEASURING

Ruler: A cork-backed steel ruler will not slip on wooden surfaces. For most miniature projects, a 12″ ruler is fine. A hobby and craft ruler with increments to ¹⁄₆₄″ would be a great help and is available in craft shops.

Pencil: Use a very sharp lead pencil to mark cutting lines on the wood. A dull point will make a thicker line, which might throw dimensions off to a noticeable degree.

T-Square: A T-square will insure accurate right angles—essential to many miniature furniture projects.

Compass: Use a compass for marking circles; remember to keep your pencil very sharp.

MISCELLANEOUS

Picks: Use a metal food pick, such as that used for nuts or shellfish, to make tiny holes.

Needles: Use sewing or knitting needles for making tiny holes in softwoods. Push needle into wood gently so as not to split the wood.

Dental Instruments: Various dental tools (if available) are wonderful for making holes, holding pieces in place, gluing, pulling pieces apart, cleaning tight areas, etc.

Sandpaper: Use extra-fine 800-grit sandpaper or the finest grit available. The finer the grit, the higher the number. Sand *with* the grain and wipe sanded surface with a soft cloth. For very small pieces, tape sandpaper to work surface and gently rub piece on it.

Emery Boards: In many cases, the fine side of an emery board can be used in place of sandpaper.

Paintbrush: Use a small paintbrush to paint or stain finished pieces. Before using brush, test to make sure the bristles will not fall out.

Q-Tips: In many cases, you can use Q-Tips to paint or stain wooden surfaces; they are also useful for reaching into tiny spaces to clean.

Jars: Small jars or cups are handy for storing and mixing paints, and are usually easier to handle than large cans.

Magnifying Glass: A magnifying glass will help in making accurate minute measurements, attaching tiny screws, painting fine details, etc.

Screwdriver: Use a jeweler's screwdriver for small screws.

Stirrers: Small plastic stirrers used for coffee or cocktails are useful for spreading glue, painting, reaching into small spaces, etc.

Tweezers: Use tweezers to hold small parts while working on them, or to pick up small components.

Materials

Remember to check the basement, attic and garage before buying any materials. Cigar-box wood, popsicle sticks, wooden matches, toothpicks and wooden spools are just a few examples of what you could use instead of buying wood for certain projects. Felt-tipped markers work as well as wood stain or paint in some cases, and clear nail polish makes a good sealer and shiner!

Below is a general look at the wood used for most miniature projects, together with some finishing ideas. Specific quantities, dimensions and any additional materials appear with each set of individual directions.

WOOD

Balsa Wood: Balsa wood is a very soft, lightweight wood that can be purchased in strips, squares and sheets starting at $\frac{1}{32}''$ thick.

Basswood: Basswood is harder than balsa wood. It can be purchased in 22″–24″ lengths in thicknesses of $\frac{1}{32}''$ up to 2″. It is also available in strips. Basswood is quite easy to work with and has a grain similar to many fine woods. It is probably the most popular wood used for making miniatures.

Hardwood Veneers: Veneers are available in a variety of grains—maple, walnut, teak, oak, cherry, mahogany, butternut, rosewood, ash, pecan, etc. Veneers are perfect for creating original miniature furniture, repairing old pieces and for covering walls and floors.

Plywood: Plywood is a hard, durable wood, available in a variety of thicknesses at lumber yards. Because plywood is usually sold in large sheets, try to buy small scrap pieces. A small handsaw is recommended for cutting plywood.

Dowels: Dowels are round wooden sticks sold at craft shops and lumber yards in 3-foot lengths and in a variety of thicknesses.

FINISHES

Acrylic Paints: For painting, acrylics are best. Apply 2 to 3 coats of paint, allowing each coat to dry thoroughly before applying the next.

Felt-tipped Pens and Markers: Felt-tipped pens and markers are excellent "paints" for small pieces of furniture or accents on larger pieces; they are available in many colors, including wood tones.

Stains: Wood stains are available in many shades; they can be brushed or rubbed onto raw wood.

Varnish and Shellac: After staining or painting, use polyurethane varnish (which is available in easy-to-use spray cans) or shellac to seal the piece and add highlights. In some cases, clear nail polish will give a shiny, hard finish.

Making Miniature Furniture from Wood

BEDS

Materials and Equipment for Each Bed (for canopy bed, see individual directions for additional materials): $\frac{1}{4}''$ plywood, 14″ × 8″ piece. Small handsaw. Fine sandpaper. White glue. Steel ruler. Rubber bands. Sharp pencil.

Directions: Refer to *Figure 1* for assembly.

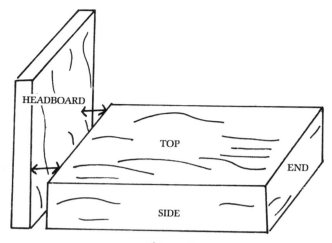

Figure 1

1. Cut the plywood into the following pieces:
   Top: one 4½″ × 6¼″ piece
   Ends: two 1″ × 4″ pieces
   Sides: two 1″ × 6¼″ pieces
   Headboard: one 4″ × 4½″ piece
2. Lightly sand any rough edges.
3. Glue ends *between* sides, keeping bottom and outer edges flush and creating a 4½″ × 6¼″ frame.
4. Glue top over frame, keeping outer edges flush; let glue dry thoroughly. If desired, nail brads around edge of top, securing top to frame.
5. Shape the headboard following individual directions, and cover with fabric following the directions on page 12. Glue headboard to one end of bed, keeping bottom edges flush. Wrap rubber bands around base of bed until glue dries.

NIGHT TABLE

Materials and Equipment: ⅛″ basswood or balsa wood, 2¾″ circle. 1½″ dowel, 1½″-long piece. White glue. Pencil. Compass.
Directions: Refer to *Figure 2* for assembly.

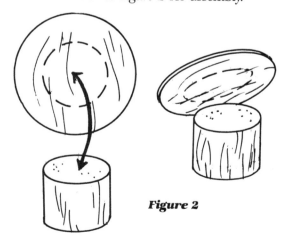

Figure 2

1. Using a compass, draw a 1½″-diameter circle in the center of the 2¾″ circle.
2. Glue dowel piece into marked circle as shown in *Figure 2*; let dry.

SCREEN

Materials and Equipment: ¼″ plywood, 6″ × 7″ piece. Four miniature brass flush or butt hinges. Pencil. Ruler. Small hand or power saw. White glue. Tiny screws and jeweler's screwdriver (optional).
Directions: Refer to *Figure 3* for assembly.

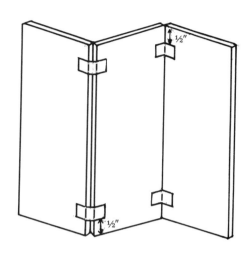

Figure 3

1. Cut plywood into three 2″ × 7″ panels. Lightly sand any rough edges. Cover panels with fabric following individual directions, or paint to match your other furnishings.
2. Attach panels to each other with brass hinges glued ½″ from ends as shown in *Figure 3*. For added support, attach hinges with screws.

CURTAIN RODS

Materials and Equipment: X-ACTO knife. Ruler. Pencil. ⅛″ wooden dowels, brass tubing or wire. Wooden or brass beads (to fit dowel, tubing or wire) for finials (jewelry findings are helpful here—look through your jewelry box or search for costume-jewelry bargains). Pins. Stain or paint, as desired. Small brushes or Q-Tips.
Directions: Refer to *Figure 4* for assembly.

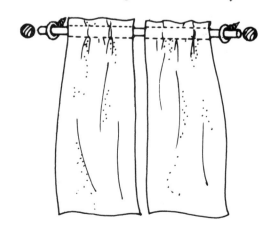

Figure 4

1. For bedroom curtains, cut dowel, tubing or wire ½″ wider than your window. For shower curtain, cut dowel, tubing or wire to appropriate size: ½″ wider than tub for straight rod or to measurement of sides and one long edge of tub for curved rod.

2. If using wooden dowels, stain or paint and let dry.

3. Using a pin, make starting holes for eye screws on each side of window frame or bathtub in appropriate position for rod. Carefully insert and screw eye screws into wood using your fingers.

4. Attach curtains to rod, then insert rod through eye screws. Attach bead finials to secure as shown in *Figure 4*.

Making Replicas of Full-Size Furniture

Making miniature versions of your own furniture is easier than you think. And wouldn't it be wonderful to hand down your own furniture, that you've made in miniature, to favorite relatives? Or how about making their furniture for them as a special gift?—it would be treasured forever. Before you start your own pieces, read the *Equipment* and *Materials* sections on pages 7–8. Practice with different woods and ways to cut them. It might be a good idea to make one or two practice pieces to get the feel of the craft before starting something as special as your own furniture. Experiment with small household tools, such as using a large sewing needle to "drill" a hole, before purchas-

ing specific ones. Once you feel ready to start, follow these steps:

1. Measure your own piece and draw it to scale on graph paper, keeping in mind that the standard scale for making and collecting miniatures is 1″ to 1′. Working in this scale will make it easier to use different sources when adding to your collection.

2. Use plywood for large, simple-shaped pieces; use either basswood or balsa wood for smaller, more delicate ones. Cut out the required shapes and sand edges lightly.

3. Stain or paint the pieces to match your own furniture. There are so many shades of wood stains and paint on the market that it would be easy to match just about any finish.

4. Once pieces are dry, glue them together and add finishing touches, drawer pulls, for example, made from links of an old necklace, small brass tacks, even bits of a toothpick. You will find that searching through "junk" drawers, jewelry boxes, garage and tag sales to find miniature treasures is just as exciting as making the actual pieces.

Once you have made a roomful of furniture, you will need a room to put them in! Containers for miniatures can range from a plywood box to a clock case. And don't overlook a small barrel cut in half, an old drawer or an antique lantern. Rummaging through the attic, thrift shops or antique stores will present you with many ideas. Use your imagination and enjoy the search.

CHAPTER 2

Miniature Sewing

Decorating miniature room settings is my favorite part of making and collecting miniatures. A paisley scarf easily becomes an "oriental" carpet, while a crocheted pot holder makes a wonderful "braided" rug. You can make a patchwork quilt from ribbons, and pretty pictures from postage stamps! You don't sew? Don't let that stop you! Many "sewn" items are really glued. A few easy hand stitches or a straight stitch on the sewing machine are all you will ever use —and if you don't have a sewing machine, the items in this book can easily be completed without one.

This chapter will help you choose the right fabrics and show you the easiest way to make miniature masterpieces. It includes general directions for all of the sewn items in this book. Specific directions appear with the individual room settings starting on page 25. As with making wooden miniatures, making fabric accessories means being prepared before you start. Always read all the directions and collect the necessary equipment and materials in your working area at once. I find it helpful to keep supplies for each project in a separate shoebox. This will not only help keep things together, but it makes the projects portable— from room to room, from house to yard, even enabling you to work while traveling.

If you have decided to reproduce your own furniture, or that of a special friend or relative as discussed in Chapter 1, you wouldn't dream of decorating with just any accessories! Get scraps of matching fabric from your bedspread and curtain hems and duplicate the whole room, providing, of course, that prints or stripes are in a small scale. If you knitted or crocheted a coverlet for your bed, do it for your miniature bed using fine yarns or threads and small hooks or needles. You can even needlepoint (sometimes called petit petitpoint) or embroider pillows or chair seats. Never think that you can't do it, just think small and improvise!

Equipment

Below is a list of the equipment you will need, not only to make the items in this book, but also for most miniature sewing projects.

Scissors: Use small, sharp embroidery scissors with a fine point to cut threads and small fabric pieces. If you are cutting a large piece of fabric, use sharp dressmaker's shears.

Needles: Use small crewel needles for embroidery and needlepoint, and sharps—medium hand-sewing needles—for just about everything else.

Pins: Use small, sharp straight pins for holding fabric in place before sewing or gluing. Do not use pins that are rusted or bent.

Thimble: Some people find wearing a thimble comfortable; I do not. However, it does protect your finger—the middle finger of your sewing hand—and it would be a good idea to get used to wearing one.

Pencil: Use a sharp pencil to mark necessary dimensions and cutting lines on fabric. For dark fabrics, use a light-colored marking pencil or a piece of sharpened tailor's chalk.

Tape Measure: A plastic tape measure is excellent. If you need smaller increments, you can carefully add them with a fine marking pen. You can also buy a hobby and craft ruler with increments to $\frac{1}{64}''$.

Ruler: Use a cork-backed steel ruler. Using a ruler instead of a tape measure might make it easier to mark dimensions on fabric.

Iron: Use a steam iron, with or without a spray. Iron all fabric pieces before measuring. A wrinkle could make a big difference in a miniature project.

Crochet Hook: Use a 00 size crochet hook to push stuffing into pillows, poke out corners, etc.

Sewing Machine: If you have a sewing machine available, it will save time. It doesn't have to include many features, because you will use only a regular straight stitch. When sewing miniatures, make 10–12 stitches per inch.

Seam Ripper: Use a seam ripper to undo mistakes or to take out basting thread. Do not pull anything out by hand.

Materials

As suggested in Chapter 1, check the materials on hand before purchasing any. Scraps of lace and sheer slips make terrific curtains, a dishcloth makes a beautiful woven coverlet! Below is a general look at most of the materials you will need for the sewing projects in this book. Specific quantities, dimensions and any additional materials appear with each set of individual directions.

Fabric: For miniature accessories, choose soft, light-weight fabrics. Light cottons, silks and linens are good choices. You might use scraps from a blouse, slip or scarf. Fancy handkerchiefs, usually sold in five-and-dime stores, make great curtains, as do scraps of old lace curtains. If you are using a patterned fabric, remember that prints should be small enough to look good in 1″ to 1′ scale. And small projects look better in light colors.

For the bath accessories, choose a thin stretch terrycloth, which is sold by the yard. You might find a washcloth or hand towel the right weight in variety or five-and-dime stores. The shower curtain? Plastic sandwich bags! And the mattresses for all the beds are made of unbleached muslin.

Trims: Trims for miniature fabric accessories can be found everywhere you look. Bits of lace, yarn, ribbon, embroidery floss, eyelet, braid and crocheted edgings are all excellent trims. Most are sold in fabric departments, but even more are probably in your sewing basket or still attached to an old curtain or piece of clothing.

Thread: Use any colorfast polyester or mercerized cotton thread to match the main color of the fabric being sewn. Be aware that washing may cause the cotton thread to shrink a bit, causing puckered seams.

Batting/Fiberfill: Use polyester fiberfill for both the pillows and quilts. It is sold loose or in sheets. Cotton batting is also available, but has the tendency to lump if the piece is washed. You can stuff pillows with cotton balls if you don't plan to wash them.

Glue: Use white Elmer's® Glue-All™ or Sobo glue to attach hems and trims. Use glue sparingly and wipe away excess with a damp cloth.

Tape: Double-faced tape will come in handy to hold curtains to window frames, bedspreads to beds, etc. You might also use masking tape to hold pieces in place while you are working on them.

Mini-Hold: This will stick fabric to wood (or to fabric) without being sticky on your hands or on the fabric. It can be used over and over again, and can be shaped, like clay, to fit anywhere. It is available in art supply and miniatures stores.

Sewing Miniature Projects
MATTRESS

Materials and Equipment for Each Mattress: Unbleached muslin, 7″ × 9½″ piece. Polyester batting, two 5″ × 7″ pieces. Thread. Sewing machine. Sewing needle. Scissors. Pins. Ruler. Crochet hook, size 00, for turning.
Directions: Refer to *Figure 5* for assembly.

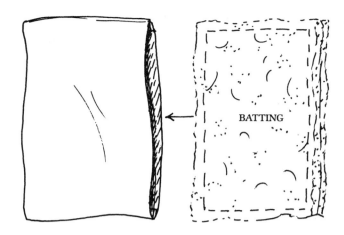

Figure 5

1. Fold muslin in half, right sides facing, to 7″ × 4¾″.

2. Machine-stitch both short edges ¼″ from raw edge. Turn piece to right side and gently push out corners with crochet hook.

3. Baste batting pieces together on all sides. Carefully insert batting into muslin cover from long open edge as shown in *Figure 5*, smoothing batting so it lies flat.

4. Turn fabric along open edge ¼″ inside; pin folded edges together. Slip-stitch opening closed.

COVERED HEADBOARD

Materials and Equipment for Each Headboard: Fabric to match bedspread or quilt, two pieces cut ½″ larger all around than wooden headboard. Polyester batting. Thread. White glue. Sewing machine. Scissors. Tape measure or ruler. Crochet hook, size 00, for turning.
Directions: Refer to *Figure 6* for assembly.

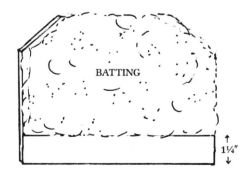

Figure 6

1. With right sides facing, machine-stitch fabric pieces together, leaving bottom edge open. Turn to right side and push out corners with crochet hook if necessary.

2. Cut layer of batting to exact shape of headboard; trim away 1¼″ from bottom edge as shown in *Figure*

6. Lightly glue batting to headboard as shown, leaving 1¼" uncovered at bottom.

3. Slip headboard into fabric cover through bottom opening, being careful not to disturb batting.

4. Glue excess fabric at bottom to wood so that wooden headboard is completely covered.

5. Glue headboard to one end of bed, with the batting side facing the bed.

SHEETS

Materials and Equipment for One Set of Sheets: Lightweight cotton fabric 45" wide, ¼ yard. Matching trim, ½" wide for top sheet, 7¾" length. Thread. Sewing machine. Scissors. Tape measure or ruler. Iron. Pins.

Directions (for bottom fitted sheet): Refer to *Figure 7* for assembly.

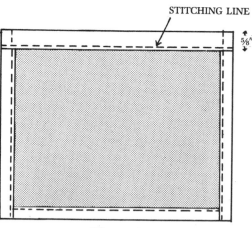

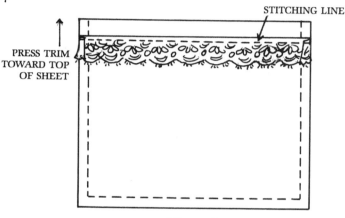

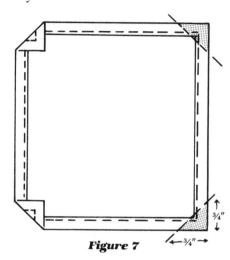

Figure 7

1. Cut a 6" × 8" piece of fabric. Fold and press all raw edges ⅛" to wrong side; machine-stitch in place.

2. Measure ¾" in from each corner and mark off four triangles as shown in *Figure 7* (shaded corners). Fold and press triangles to wrong side of sheet as shown in *Figure 7*.

3. Bring folded edges of one triangle together with right sides facing. Make a ⅛" seam starting from the corner point and stitching toward the edge of the fabric. This will form a pocket in which to fit the mattress. Repeat on remaining corners. Turn corners to right side and press along the ¾" fold thus formed all around the entire edge of the sheet. Place sheet on mattress.

Directions (for top sheet): Refer to *Figures 8* and *9* for assembly.

1. Cut an 8"-square piece of fabric. Fold and press three edges ⅛" to the wrong side twice. Machine-stitch in place.

2. Turn unstitched edge ⅛" to wrong side and press. Turn again ⅝". Press and stitch as shown in *Figure 8*.

3. Turn raw edges of trim ⅛" to wrong side and stitch. With right sides facing, pin trim to sheet over

Figure 8

Figure 9

stitching line as shown in *Figure 9*. Stitch in place along first stitching line.

4. Press trim toward folded top of sheet following the arrow in *Figure 9*. Place sheet on mattress, trim side down. Fold top of sheet back 1½", exposing trimmed edge; tuck edges of top sheet neatly under mattress.

BEDCOVERS

The five beds shown in this book are about 4½" × 6½"; all directions are based on these measurements. If your own miniature bed is a different size, adjust the given measurements accordingly. Remember that all designs can also be hand-sewn, following the same directions.

Equipment for All: Sewing machine. Sewing needle. Scissors. Tape measure or ruler. Iron. Pins. Marking pencil. Crochet hook, size 00, for turning.

Bedspreads

Materials for Each Bedspread: Lightweight fabric, 8¼" × 8" piece, in light solid color or small-scale print. Ruffled eyelet or lace trim 1" wide, ¾ yard. Thread.

Directions: Refer to *Figure 10* for assembly.

Figure 10

1. Place fabric wrong side up on work surface with 8″ dimension at top and bottom. Fold bottom and side edges ¼″ to wrong side and press.

2. Turn top edge of fabric ⅛″ to wrong side and press. Turn again ⅛″ to wrong side; press and stitch in place.

3. Cut two lengths of trim for sides, each 8¾″, and one length for bottom, 6½″. Fold raw edges of each piece of trim ¼″ to wrong side and press. Position straight edge of trim beneath pressed edge of fabric so trim extends beyond fabric as shown in *Figure 10*. Topstitch close to edge, securing each length of trim to fabric.

BEDSPREAD VARIATIONS

1. If your bed has a footboard or posts as in the canopy bed on page 36, cut an approximate 1½″ square from each bottom corner as shown in *Figure 11*. Turn raw edges ⅛″ to wrong side and stitch. Use double-faced tape or mini-hold to secure spread to bed.

2. If you have a box bed similar to any of the beds in this book, you can box the bottom corners of your spread as follows: Sew trim to the spread, ending ⅜″

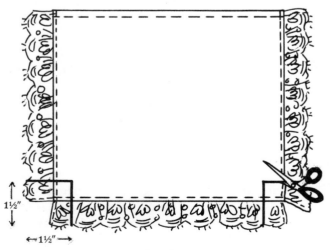

1½″

←1½″→

Figure 11

from the corners as shown in *Figure 12*. Fold and sew each bottom corner of spread as shown in *Figure 13*. Turn to right side and shape corners as shown in *Figure 14*.

⅜″

⅜″

Figure 12

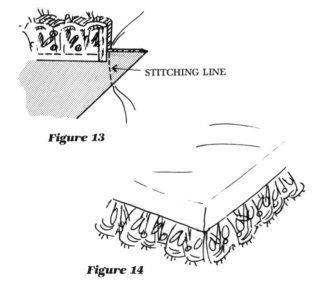

STITCHING LINE

Figure 13

Figure 14

Quilts

Materials for Each Quilt: Lightweight fabric, 15″ × 7½″ piece, in light solid color or small-scale print. Polyester fiberfill, 7″ square. Thread.

Directions: Refer to *Figure 15* for assembly.

1. Cut fabric into two 7½″ squares. Center batting on wrong side of one fabric square and pin. Baste batting in place around all edges.

2. With right sides facing, machine-stitch fabric squares together, ¼″ in from edges, leaving a 2″ opening at center bottom.

3. Turn quilt to right side without disturbing batting and gently push corners out with crochet hook. Fold raw edges of opening ¼″ inside and slip-stitch opening closed.

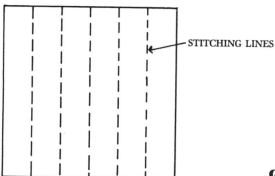

Figure 15

4. On one side of quilt, use tailor's chalk to lightly mark parallel lines 1″ apart as shown in *Figure 15*. Machine-stitch along each line.

QUILT VARIATIONS

1. If you wish to include eyelet or lace trim around edges of quilt, pin and stitch trim to second fabric piece (first piece has batting), with right sides facing and raw edges even, easing trim around corners. Continue from step 2, above. When folding raw edges inside while finishing quilt, allow trim to extend beyond opening; slip-stitch opening closed.

2. If you choose a print fabric with a striped design, use the vertical design lines as quilting lines for an interesting effect.

PILLOWS

There are many different pillows shown throughout this book. They each fall into one of four basic groups; general directions for these groups follow. Specific variations are given with the individual directions. Remember that you can make all of the pillows without a sewing machine. See *Figure 16* for length and width, as used below.

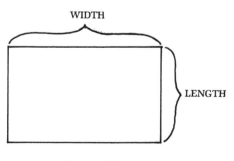

Figure 16

Materials and Equipment for All Pillows: Two fabric scraps, no more than 3″ square. Fiberfill (or cotton balls). Trim if desired. Thread. Sewing machine. Sewing needle. Scissors. Tape measure or ruler. Iron. Pins. Marking pencil. Crochet hook, size 00, for turning.

ILLUSTRATION 1

Group A

Pillowcase stuffer or plain, untrimmed pillow; see *Illustration 1*.
Directions: Refer to *Figure 17* for assembly.

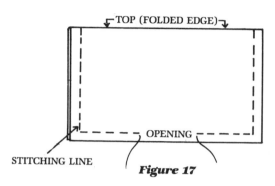

Figure 17

1. Decide upon desired finished size of pillow. Cut fabric ½″ more than width and double-plus-½″ the length of the pillow.

2. Fold fabric in half lengthwise with right sides facing. Stitch ¼″ from sides and bottom, leaving a 1″ opening at bottom center as shown in *Figure 17*.

3. Turn pillow to right side, gently pushing out corners with a crochet hook. Carefully stuff to desired firmness with fiberfill or cotton balls. Fold raw edges of opening ¼″ inside and slip-stitch opening closed.

ILLUSTRATION 2

Group B

Trimmed pillowcase; see *Illustration 2*.
Directions: Refer to *Figures 18–19* for assembly.

1. Decide upon desired finished size of pillowcase. Cut fabric ¾″ more than width and double-plus-½″ desired length of pillowcase. Cut trim same length as fabric piece.

15

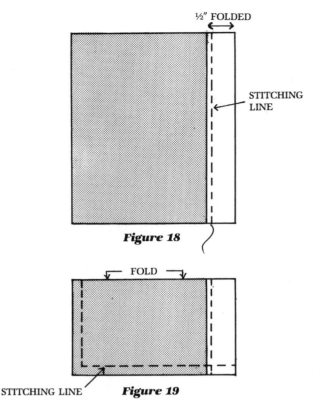

Figure 18

Figure 19

STITCHING LINE

2. Fold one side edge of fabric ½″ to wrong side and stitch; see *Figure 18*.

3. Pin trim to right side of fabric over stitching line, with finished edge of trim facing fold; stitch in place.

4. Fold fabric in half lengthwise, right sides facing, and stitch ¼″ from raw edges on two sides as shown in *Figure 19*.

5. Turn pillowcase to right side, gently pushing corners out with crochet hook.

ILLUSTRATION 3

Group C

Pillow trimmed all around with lace or eyelet; see *Illustration 3*.

Directions:

1. Decide upon desired finished size of pillow. Cut two fabric pieces ½″ wider and longer than pillow. Measure perimeter of one piece of fabric and cut length of trim ½″ longer than perimeter.

2. Pin trim to one piece of fabric with right sides facing and raw edges even, easing trim around corners. Finished edges of trim will face center of fabric piece. Overlap or turn cut edges of trim under where they meet. Baste trim in place, ¼″ from edges.

3. Place fabric pieces together, right sides facing, and stitch ¼″ from edges, leaving a 1″ opening at center bottom.

4. Turn pillow to right side exposing trim, and gently push corners out with a crochet hook. Carefully stuff to desired firmness. Turn raw edges of fabric opening ¼″ inside, leaving trim free, and slip-stitch opening closed.

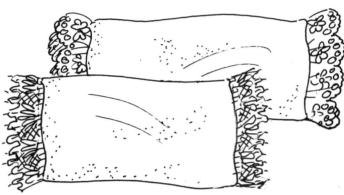

ILLUSTRATION 4

Group D

Pillows trimmed with lace or eyelet on two sides; see *Illustration 4*.

Directions: Refer to *Figure 20* for assembly.

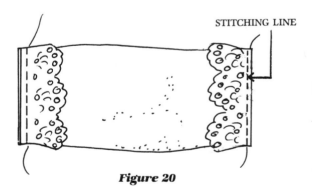

STITCHING LINE

Figure 20

1. Decide upon desired finished size of pillow. Cut fabric ½″ more than width and double-plus-½″ length of pillow. Cut two pieces of trim, each the same length as the fabric.

2. Pin trim along length of fabric with right sides facing and raw edges even; machine-stitch ¼″ from raw edges as shown in *Figure 20*; finished edges of trim will face center of fabric piece.

3. Fold fabric in half lengthwise with right sides facing, and stitch all around edges; make a ¼″ seam and leave an opening at center bottom.

4. Turn pillow to right side exposing trim, and gently push out corners with a crochet hook. Carefully stuff to desired firmness. Turn raw edges of fabric opening ¼″ inside and slip-stitch opening closed.

WINDOW CURTAINS

The following directions are for curtains consisting of two panels per window, each panel measuring 7″ × 4″. They are meant to just reach the floor and can be tied back as shown in the photographs of the room settings. Adjust the measurements to fit your own windows as necessary. Remember that a sewing machine is not necessary to make any of the curtains. **Materials and Equipment for All Curtains:** Fabric, about 12″ square, to match or contrast with your bedspread or quilt. Trim, about ¾ yard, if desired. Thread. Sewing machine. Sewing needle. Scissors. Tape measure or ruler. Pins. Marking pencil. Iron.
Directions: Refer to *Figure 21* for assembly.

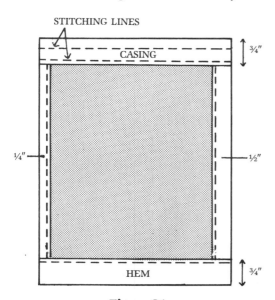

Figure 21

1. Cut two fabric panels, 8¾″ × 5″. Turn all raw edges ⅛″ to wrong side and press.

2. Turn one long edge of each panel ¼″ to wrong side and stitch for outside edge. Turn opposite long edge of each panel ½″ to wrong side and stitch for inside edge.

3. For top casing, turn fabric ¾″ to wrong side and stitch close to edge. Stitch again ¼″ from top as shown in *Figure 21*.

4. For hem, turn fabric ¾″ to wrong side and stitch. Repeat procedure for second panel, making sure that side measurements are reversed.

5. Follow individual directions with each room setting or variation for making tiebacks for the curtains.
CURTAIN VARIATIONS

1. To trim the inside edges of curtain panels, cut two pieces of trim, each 8¾″ long. Pin trim to one inside edge of a curtain panel with right sides facing and raw edges even so finished edge of trim faces center of panel. Stitch trim in place ¼″ from the edge. Fold trim *away* from the curtain panel and press. Topstitch close to edge of curtain, securing trim. Complete curtain as described above.

2. For lace curtains, use 4″-wide lace with a scalloped edge for your fabric. Position the scallops along each inside edge, then follow steps 3 and 4 above for the top casing and hem.

3. To make "puff draperies," cut fabric panels 14¾″ × 4″ and follow step 1 above; for curtains with less puff, cut shorter panels. Make ⅛″ side hems. Follow steps 3 and 4 above for the top casing and hem. For tiebacks, cut two 9″ × ½″ strips of matching or contrasting fabric. Turn long raw edges ⅛″ to wrong side twice and stitch, forming a ¼″ band. Cut each fabric strip in half, making four 4½″ × ¼″ tiebacks. Fold short raw edges to wrong side and stitch in place. Place panels on curtain rod; tie following *Figure 22*.

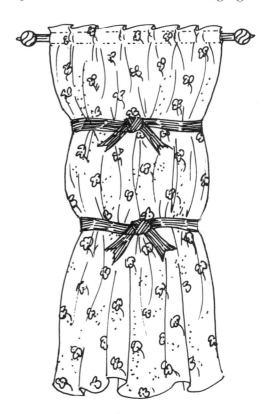

Figure 22

CHAPTER 3

Bath Ensembles

The following pages show two collections for decorating a miniature bathroom. Both include a robe, slippers, bathmat and a set of five towels. The second collection also includes a shower curtain that can easily be adapted to any bathroom. Be sure to read the *Equipment* and *Materials* sections in Chapter 2 and the *General Directions for Terrycloth Bath Accessories* that follow before starting to work. Specific amounts and colors for fabric and trim are included in the individual directions.

General Directions for Terrycloth Bath Accessories

Materials and Equipment for All Accessories: Small amounts of lightweight stretch terrycloth fabric. Ribbon or lace trim ⅜″ or ½″ wide, about ½ yard. Felt scrap for slipper soles. Thread. Sewing machine. Sewing needle. Scissors. Pins. Ruler. Tracing paper for patterns.

Directions for Bathrobe: Refer to *Figures 23–24* for assembly.

1. Cut a 4½″ × 7½″ piece of terrycloth. Also from terrycloth, cut a strip for belt, ½″ × 7½″.

2. Fold large fabric piece in half to 4½″ × 3¾″.

3. Trace bathrobe pattern and use to cut out bathrobe following *Figure 23* for placement on folded fabric; note that the rounded neck edge of the pattern extends beyond the fabric. Keeping the pattern pinned to one half of the fabric, open out the cut fabric piece and follow the dot/dash lines on the pattern to cut the neck and center front openings.

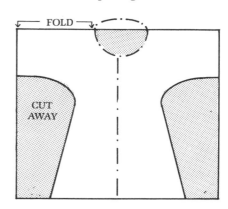

Figure 23

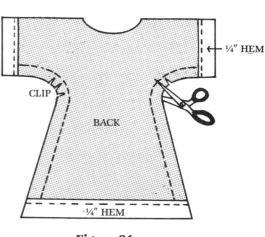

Figure 24

4. Turn fabric ¼″ to wrong side along hem and sleeve edges; stitch. Fold robe in half, right sides facing, and stitch underarm and side seams ¼″ from edges; clip as shown in *Figure 24*.

PATTERN FOR BATHROBE

5. Turn center front and neck edge of bathrobe ¼″ to wrong side; stitch. Turn robe to right side.

6. Fold belt in half lengthwise, right sides facing; stitch close to long edge. Turn to right side; tie around robe.

Directions for Bathmat: Refer to *Figure 25* for assembly.

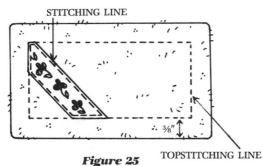

STITCHING LINE

⅜″

TOPSTITCHING LINE

Figure 25

1. Cut two 2½″ × 3¾″ pieces of terrycloth. With right sides facing, stitch pieces together ¼″ from the edge around all sides, leaving an opening for turning.

2. Clip corners; turn mat to right side. Fold raw edges inside and slip-stitch opening closed. Topstitch ⅜″ from all sides as shown in *Figure 25*.

3. Cut a piece of trim 2½″ long and stitch to mat around all sides as shown in *Figure 25*. Clip away excess trim at ends.

Directions for Slippers: Refer to *Figure 26* for assembly.

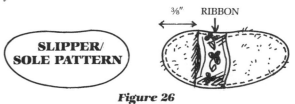

⅜″   RIBBON

SLIPPER/ SOLE PATTERN

Figure 26

1. Trace slipper/sole pattern and use to cut out two terrycloth slippers and two felt soles. Cut two 1″ lengths of ribbon.

2. Pin ribbon to right side of each terrycloth slipper as shown in *Figure 26*; pin felt sole to wrong side of slipper. Stitch terrycloth slipper to felt sole, catching ribbon edges in the line of stitching. Trim away any excess ribbon, even with the edge of the slipper.

Directions for Towels:

1. Cut terrycloth ¼″ wider and ½″ longer than desired size of towel.

2. Turn fabric ⅛″ to wrong side on both long side edges and stitch close to raw edges. Turn ¼″ to wrong side at top and bottom edges and stitch in same manner.

3. Cut trim to fit across towel and pin to right side, ⅜″ from bottom; topstitch both long edges of trim in place.

VELVET AND LACE FOR THE BATH

Materials: Lightweight beige terrycloth, ¼ yard. Velvet ribbon ¼″ wide, ½ yard lavender. Ecru lace trim ¾″ wide, ⅓ yard. Scrap of beige or tan felt. Thread.

ROBE, SLIPPERS AND MAT

Follow the *General Directions* to make the robe, slippers and bathmat, using beige terrycloth for all and beige or tan felt for slipper soles. Trim the slippers and bathmat with lavender velvet ribbon.

TOWELS

1. Follow the *General Directions* to make the following towels, using beige terrycloth:
  one bath towel, 4½″ long × 4¼″ wide
  two hand towels, 3¼″ long × 2½″ wide
  one fingertip towel, 2½″ long × 2″ wide
2. To trim towels, pin raw edge of lace under velvet ribbon before you stitch, so that the finished edge of the lace falls slightly below the bottom edge of the towel as shown in *Figure 27*.

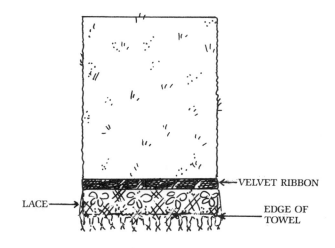

Figure 27

FLOWERED BATH SET

Shown in color on the back cover

Materials: Lightweight orange terrycloth, 4½″ × 7½″ piece. Lightweight yellow terrycloth, ¼ yard. Flowered ribbon ⅜″ wide, 1½ yards. Scrap of yellow felt. Thread to match terrycloth, and white. Two clear plastic sandwich bags with flap (rather than zip-lock) closing. ⅛″-diameter dowel, 9″ length, or medium-weight wire.

ROBE, SLIPPERS AND MAT

Follow the *General Directions* to make the robe, slippers and bathmat, using orange terrycloth for the robe, yellow terrycloth for the slippers and mat, and yellow felt for the slipper soles. Trim the slippers and bathmat with flowered ribbon.

TOWELS

1. Follow the *General Directions* to make the following towels, using yellow terrycloth:

one bath towel, 4½″ long × 4¼″ wide
two hand towels, 3¼″ long × 2½″ wide
one fingertip towel, 2½″ long × 2″ wide
2. Trim towels with flowered ribbon.

SHOWER CURTAINS

1. Carefully cut off flap from top of one plastic sandwich bag. The remaining folded edge of the bag will become the casing for the shower-curtain rod; clip this flap at each side edge so flap lifts up freely. You will now have a 5½″ square of doubled plastic with a single layer of plastic extending above it; this will be the top of the shower curtain.

2. Pin ribbon to plastic ¼″ away from side and bottom edges; miter ribbon at the corner and turn raw ends under ¼″ as shown in *Figure 28*. Topstitch both long edges of ribbon with matching thread.

3. Fold top (single layer) of plastic ½″ to wrong side

22

and stitch close to fold using white thread. Stitch again close to lower edge of flap as shown in *Figure 29*, forming casing for shower curtain rod.

4. Repeat with a second plastic bag, reversing trim as shown in *Figure 30*.

5. For shower-curtain rod, see page 9.

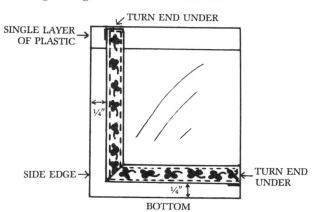

Figure 28

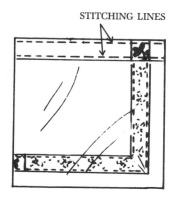

Figure 29

Figure 30

Bedroom Ensembles

ROMANTIC REVERSAL BOUDOIR ENSEMBLE

Shown in color on the front cover, fabric by Laura Ashley

This boudoir ensemble uses a delicate white-on-blue print for the headboard, spread, quilt and curtains. Reverse it to blue-on-white for the folding screen and night table to capture a gentle, romantic look. Be sure to read Chapters 1 and 2 for basic equipment and materials before beginning.

Materials (for headboard cover, screen and table covers, bedspread, pillows, quilt and curtains): *Fabric:* Lightweight cotton white-on-blue print 45″ wide, ½ yard. Blue-on-white print (reverse of above) 45″ wide, ¼ yard. White cotton, 6″ × 7″ piece. White-on-white "textured" cotton, one 6″ × 7″ and one 6″ by 5″ piece. White cotton sateen or polished cotton, 2″ × 4″ piece. *Trims:* White ruffled eyelet trim: 1⅜″ wide, ¾ yard; ⅜″ wide, 1½ yards. White lace trim ⅜″ wide, ¼ yard. White twill tape or ribbon ¼″ wide, 1½ yards. White cord ⅛″ wide, ¼ yard. *Miscellaneous:* Thread to match fabric and trims. Batting and fiberfill. Paints or markers for designer pillow. Glue.

BED

1. Make box bed and headboard following directions on page 8; make headboard 3½″ × 4½″.

2. Cover headboard following directions on page 12, using white-on-blue fabric. Then:

A. Cut a strip of same fabric 20″ × 1″. Fold and press all raw edges ¼″ to wrong side.

B. Machine-baste close to both long edges. Pull bobbin thread to gather strip to 10¾″ length.

C. Pin gathered strip around front edge of headboard as shown in *Figure 31*; slip-stitch in place.

D. Glue headboard to bed as directed on page 9.

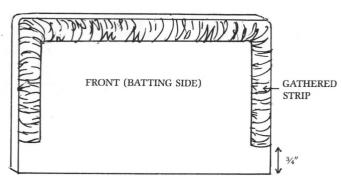

FRONT (BATTING SIDE)

GATHERED STRIP

¾″

Figure 31

BEDDING

1. Make mattress following directions on page 12.

2. Make bedspread following directions on page 13, using white-on-blue fabric and 1⅜″- wide eyelet trim, *except* cut fabric 2″ narrower and 1″ shorter than directed.

3. Make five pillows:

A. Make two pillows 2″ × 1¼″, following Group C directions on page 16, using 6″ × 7″ piece of white-on-white "textured" fabric and ⅜″ eyelet trim.

B. Make one pillow 2⅝″ × 1⅛″, following Group C directions on page 16, using white-on-blue fabric and ⅜″ eyelet trim.

C. Make one pillow 1⅝″ × 1⅜″, following Group D directions on page 16, using 6″ × 5″ piece of white-on-white "textured" fabric and ⅜″ eyelet trim.

D. Make one pillow 2⅛″ × 1⅜″, following Group C directions on page 16, using white sateen or polished cotton fabric and lace trim. Before assembling pillow, paint flowers, or any other design, onto right side of one fabric piece, using acrylic paint or markers; be sure to check markers for bleeding before using. Keep design centered so it does not extend into seam allowance.

4. Make quilt following directions on page 14 and below:

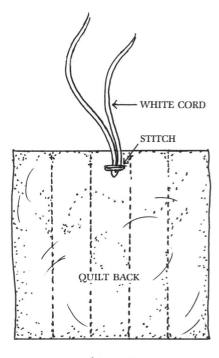

WHITE CORD

STITCH

QUILT BACK

Figure 32

A. Cut top piece from white-on-blue fabric and backing from solid white, each 5½″ × 6½″. Cut batting 5″ × 6″. Finish quilt as directed.

B. Fold white cord in half and stitch to center top of quilt back as shown in *Figure 32*.

C. Roll quilt printed side out, starting at the bottom, and tie with the white cord to secure. Place quilt at foot of bed as shown in the photograph.

CURTAINS

1. Make curtains following directions on page 17, using white-on-blue fabric and ⅜″ eyelet trim. Then:

A. Cut two additional pieces of eyelet trim the width of curtain panels; turn raw edges to wrong side and press. Topstitch trim to curtain, beneath rod casing as shown in *Figure 33*.

2. For tiebacks, cut two 4″ pieces of ⅜″ eyelet trim; turn long raw edges ⅛″ to wrong side twice and stitch.

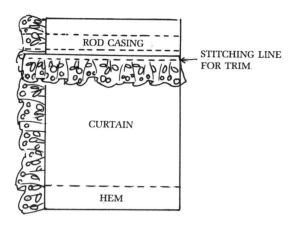

ROD CASING

STITCHING LINE
FOR TRIM.

CURTAIN

HEM

Figure 33

3. Tie curtains back as shown in the photograph; overlap ends of tieback slightly in back and stitch to hold.

4. For curtain rods, see page 9.

SCREEN

1. Make screen following directions on page 9. Then:

A. Glue blue-on-white fabric to both sides of each panel so the fabric wraps ⅛″ over the edges of each panel.

B. Starting at base of one long side edge, wrap and glue twill tape or ribbon along side, over top and down along opposite side of each panel covering raw edges of fabric.

C. Hinge panels as directed.

NIGHT TABLE

1. Make night table following directions on page 9. Then:

A. Cut strip of blue-on-white fabric to fit around table base, overlapping ends; glue in place.

B. Cut 4½″-diameter circle of blue-on-white fabric; glue table top to center of wrong side of fabric.

C. Following *Figure 34*, wrap and glue excess fabric beneath table top, pleating with your fingers at even intervals to take up excess fabric.

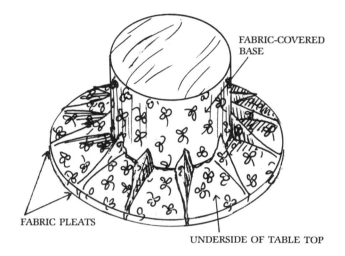

FABRIC-COVERED BASE

FABRIC PLEATS

UNDERSIDE OF TABLE TOP

Figure 34

COUNTRY FLOWERS BEDROOM

Shown in color on the inside front cover

This cheerful setting will look charming in any dollhouse. A country print quilt and overstuffed pillows sit on crisp yellow bedsheets that are trimmed with eyelet. Headboard, folding screen and cool white curtains repeat the flowered print for a double helping of country charm. Be sure to read Chapters 1 and 2 for basic equipment and materials before beginning.

Materials (for bed, headboard and screen covers, sheets, quilt, pillows and curtains): *Fabric:* Floral ticking or cotton with a floral/stripe design 45″ wide, ½ yard. Solid yellow (or color to match floral) cotton 45″ wide, ¼ yard. White cotton, 12″ × 12″ piece. Muslin, 6″ × 6″ piece. *Trims:* White ruffled eyelet trim ½″ wide, 1½ yards. White flat eyelet ½″ wide, ¾ yard. White twill tape or ribbon ¼″ wide, 1½ yards. *Miscellaneous:* Thread to match fabric and trims. Batting and fiberfill. Glue.

BED

1. Make box bed and headboard following directions on page 8; make headboard 3½″ × 4½″.

2. Cut solid yellow fabric to cover top and three sides of bed. Glue fabric to bed.

3. Cover and attach headboard to uncovered end of bed following directions on pages 12 and 9, using floral fabric.

BEDDING

1. Make mattress following directions on page 12.

2. Make top and bottom sheets following directions on page 13, using solid yellow fabric and flat eyelet trim.

3. Make quilt following directions on page 14, using floral fabric and ruffled eyelet trim. Position stripes so they run the *length* of the quilt.

4. Make four pillows:

A. Make two pillows 2¾″ × 2″, following Group A directions on page 15, using floral fabric.

B. Make two pillowcase stuffers 1″ × 2″, following Group A directions on page 15, using muslin.

C. Make two pillowcases 1⅜″ × 2⅝″, following Group B directions on page 16, using solid yellow fabric and flat eyelet trim.

CURTAINS

1. Make curtains following directions on page 17, using plain white fabric and ruffled eyelet trim—except, before turning fabric to wrong side for casing and hem, cut a strip of floral fabric 1¼″ wide and 8¾″ long for each panel, cutting the strip of fabric to take advantage of the stripe pattern. Turn long edges of the strip ⅛″ to wrong side and press. Pin strip along inner edge of panel as shown in *Figure 35*.

2. For each tieback:

A. Cut a ¾″ × 5½″ piece of floral fabric (again utilizing the stripe pattern) and a 5½″ piece of flat eyelet trim; turn long edges of floral fabric ¼″ to

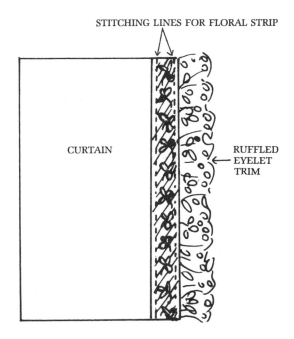

STITCHING LINES FOR FLORAL STRIP

CURTAIN

RUFFLED EYELET TRIM

Figure 35

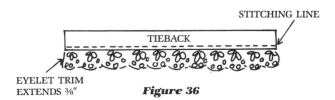

STITCHING LINE

TIEBACK

EYELET TRIM EXTENDS ⅜″   *Figure 36*

wrong side and stitch. Repeat for short edges of floral fabric and eyelet.

B. Fold floral fabric in half lengthwise, right side out; place unfinished edge of trim between.

C. Stitch close to edge of floral fabric as shown in *Figure 36*, securing trim.

3. Tie curtain back as shown in the photograph, overlapping ends of tieback slightly behind curtain; slip-stitch to hold.

4. For curtain rods, see page 9.

SCREEN

1. Make screen following directions on page 9. Then:

A. Glue floral fabric to both sides of each panel so the fabric wraps ⅛″ over the edges of each panel.

B. Starting at base of one long side edge, wrap and glue twill tape or ribbon along side, over top and down along opposite side of each panel, covering raw edges of fabric.

C. Hinge panels as directed.

SATIN AND LACE BEDROOM
Shown in color on the inside front cover

Here is a lesson in combining the traditional look of satin with the airiness of lace. The main fabric is a pale yellow crepe with a subtle sheen; the spread and pillows are trimmed with white lace; the curtains are made of sheer white lace. Be sure to read Chapters 1 and 2 for basic equipment and materials before beginning.

Materials (for headboard cover, bedspread, pillows and curtains): *Fabric:* Yellow satin-backed crepe 45″ wide, ¼ yard. *Trims:* White lace trim with scalloped edge 4″ wide, ½ yard. White ruffled lace ⅜″ wide, 1½ yards. White satin ribbon with lace edging 1″ wide, 2″ length. White flat lace trim ⅜″ wide, ½ yard. *Miscellaneous:* Thread to match fabric and trims. Batting and fiberfill. Tracing paper.

BED

1. Make box bed and headboard following directions on page 8; trace headboard pattern and use to cut one headboard from ¼″ plywood.

2. Cover and attach headboard following directions on pages 12 and 9, using yellow crepe.

BEDDING

1. Make mattress following directions on page 12.

2. Make bedspread following directions on page 13, using yellow crepe and ⅜″-wide ruffled lace trim. Then pin two pieces of flat lace trim down length of spread, 1¼″ from each side as shown in *Figure 37*. Topstitch long edge of each in place.

3. Make five pillows:

   A. Make two pillows 2″ square, following Group C directions on page 16, using yellow crepe and ⅜″-wide ruffled lace trim.

   B. Make two pillows 1¾″ × 1″, following Group D directions on page 16, using yellow crepe and ⅜″-wide ruffled lace trim, doubled.

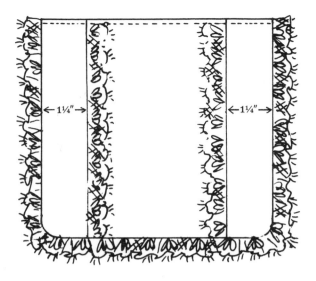

Figure 37

   C. Make one pillow 2½″ × 1½″, following Group C directions on page 16, using yellow crepe and narrow lace trim, except before stitching pillow pieces together, center and pin satin ribbon with lace trim to right side of one fabric piece; catch ends of ribbon in the seam allowance as you stitch.

CURTAINS

1. Make curtains following directions on page 17, using wide scalloped lace for fabric.

2. For curtain rods, see page 9.

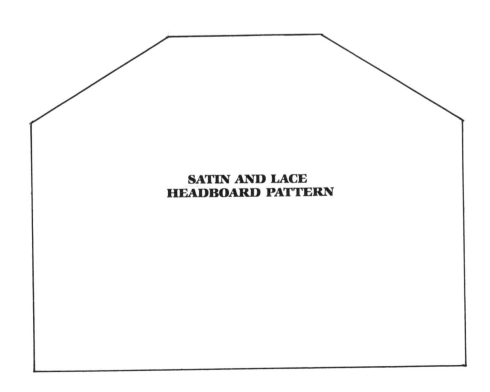

**SATIN AND LACE
HEADBOARD PATTERN**

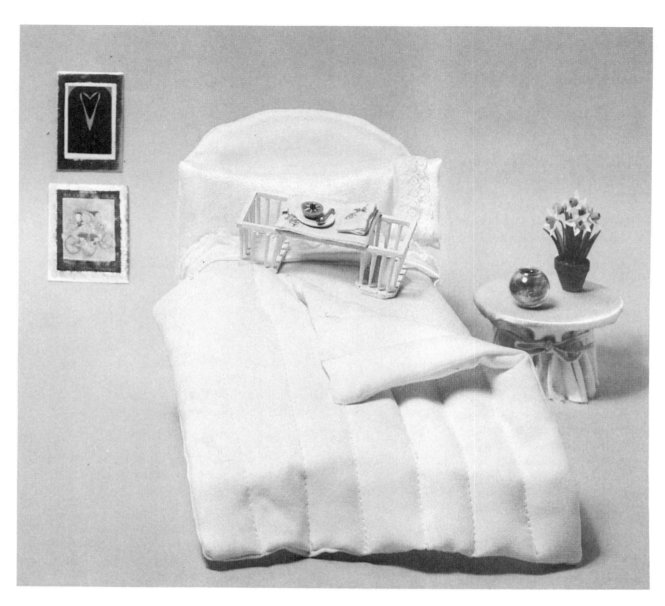

WHITE SATIN NIGHTS
Shown in color on the inside back cover

White satin sheets, crepe-covered headboard, plush comforter and pillows—all
white and dreamy and irresistible. Add satin curtains and table cover for a
feeling of wraparound luxury. Be sure to read Chapters 1 and 2 for basic equipment and materials before beginning.

Materials (for bed, headboard and table covers, sheets, quilt, pillows and curtains): *Fabric:* White satin-backed crepe 45″ wide, ¼ yard. White silk crepe 45″ wide, ¼ yard. Muslin, 4″ × 5″ piece. White cotton, 6″ × 6″ piece. *Trims:* White ruffled lace trim ½″ wide, ¾ yard. White cord, 12″ length. *Miscellaneous:* Thread to match fabric and trims. Batting and fiberfill. Glue. Four buttons for bed feet, 1″ diameter, rounded on one side and about ½″ thick. Tracing paper. Compass. Pinking shears. Mini-hold.

BED

1. Make box bed and headboard following directions on page 8; trace headboard pattern and use to cut one headboard from ¼″ plywood.

2. Cut white silk crepe to cover top and three sides of bed. Glue fabric to bed.

3. Cover and attach headboard to uncovered end of bed following directions on pages 12 and 9, using white silk crepe.

4. Cut four 3″-diameter circles from white silk crepe. Cover each button as follows:

    A. Place button, rounded side down, centered on wrong side of fabric circle.

    B. Gather fabric to back (flat) side of button and glue ends smoothly in place.

    C. Glue back of each button to bottom of bed, slightly in from each corner.

BEDDING

1. Make mattress following directions on page 12.

2. Make top and bottom sheets following directions on page 13, using white satin crepe and lace trim—except, trim top sheet with two rows of lace, the top row covering the stitching line of the bottom row as shown in *Figure 38*.

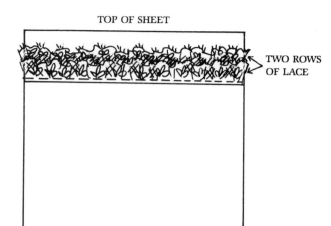

TOP OF SHEET

TWO ROWS OF LACE

Figure 38

3. Make quilt following directions on page 14, using white silk crepe. Note: Turned-back corner of quilt shown in photograph is stitched to quilt top.

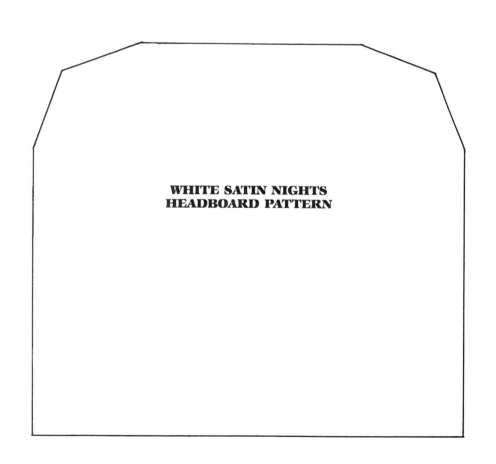

WHITE SATIN NIGHTS HEADBOARD PATTERN

4. Make two pillows:

A. Make one pillowcase stuffer 4″ × 1½″, following Group A directions on page 15, using muslin.

B. Make one pillowcase 4¾″ × 1¾″, following Group B directions on page 15, using white satin crepe and two rows of lace trim.

CURTAINS

Note: Curtains are not shown in the photograph.

1. Make curtains following directions on page 17, using white satin.

2. For each tieback:

A. Trace tieback pattern and use to cut one piece from white satin crepe and one piece from white cotton.

B. Stitch each cotton tieback to a satin one with right sides facing, leaving an opening for turning.

C. Turn to right side and slip-stitch opening closed; press.

3. Tie curtain back overlapping ends of tieback slightly behind curtain; slip-stitch to hold.

4. For curtain rods, see page 9.

Figure 39

NIGHT TABLE

1. Make night table following directions on page 9. Then:

A. Use compass to draw a circle on white satin crepe, 7″ in diameter. Cut out using pinking shears.

B. Cover table base with mini-hold. Center and glue fabric circle over top of table. Wrap fabric evenly over edge of table top and attach to table base, arranging folds and securing them with mini-hold as shown in *Figure 39*.

C. When satisfied with folds around table base, tie white cord around upper portion of base as shown in the photograph, making a bow.

WHITE SATIN NIGHTS
TIEBACK PATERN

CONTEMPORARY CANOPY BEDROOM SET

Shown in color on the inside back cover

Create excitement with a contemporary variation of a traditional theme. This white canopy bed whispers simplicity and elegance with white spread and pillows trimmed with contrasting floral print. Dark floral draperies and covered lampshade, however, ignite the dramatic fuse for a perfect balance. Be sure to read Chapters 1 and 2 for basic equipment and materials before beginning.

Materials (for bedspread, pillows, curtains and lampshade cover): **Fabric:** Lightweight white gabardine 45″ wide, ¼ yard. White cotton, 8″ × 9″ piece. Dark floral cotton print 45″ wide, ¼ yard. **Miscellaneous:** Thread to match fabrics. Fiberfill. Tracing paper. **Materials** (for canopy bed): ¼″ basswood or plywood, one sheet. ⅛″ basswood, one sheet. ¼″-square basswood strip, one 24″ piece and one 28″ piece. White paint. Clear varnish or polyurethane. Glue. Small nails.

BED

1. Cut the following pieces for bed:

Top: one 4½″ × 6¼″ piece from ⅛″ basswood sheet

Ends: two 4″ × 1¼″ pieces from ¼″ basswood or plywood sheet

Sides: two 5¾″ × 1¼″ pieces from ¼″ basswood or plywood sheet

Headboard: one 4½″ × 2⅝″ piece from ⅛″ basswood sheet

Canopy Top: two 4″ pieces and two 6¼″ pieces from ¼″ basswood strip (24″)

Posts: four 7″ pieces from ¼″ basswood strip (28″)

2. For top, carefully cut out a ¼″-square notch in each corner as shown in *Figure 40.*

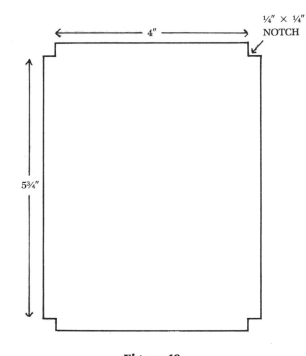

Figure 40

3. To make bed frame, glue posts to short edges of each side piece with bottom edges flush as shown in *Figure 41.*

4. Glue ends *between* posts, again keeping bottom

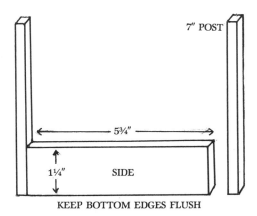

7″ POST

5¾″

1¼″   SIDE

KEEP BOTTOM EDGES FLUSH

Figure 41

edges flush; this will form the rectangular frame of the bed. For added support, carefully nail each post to sides and ends, about ½″ from bottom of bed.

5. Run glue around top edges of bed frame, then carefully lower top piece onto frame and press to secure; all outer edges should be flush. Allow glue to dry. Refer to *Figure 42.*

6. Glue headboard behind posts at one end of bed, keeping all edges flush; let dry. Nail headboard to posts about ½″ from bottom of bed.

7. For canopy top, glue 4″ strips *between* 6¼″ strips; let dry thoroughly between coats. When dry, glue, then nail canopy to posts, keeping edges flush.

8. Paint bed white, using two or three coats of paint if necessary, and letting paint dry between coats. When final coat is dry, finish with clear varnish or polyurethane; let dry thoroughly.

BEDDING

1. Make mattress following directions on page 12.

2. Make bedspread as follows:

A. Trace bedspread pattern on page 38 and use to cut one bedspread from white gabardine and one backing from white cotton fabric. From floral fabric, cut ½″-wide strips for trim, to fit positions indicated on bedspread pattern.

B. Fold long raw edges of trim ⅛″ to wrong side and press. Pin to bedspread as indicated on pattern with raw ends of trim matching raw edges of fabric. Miter corners where necessary; topstitch all long edges in place.

C. With right sides facing and raw edges even, stitch backing to bedspread ¼″ from edges, leaving an opening for turning; turn to right side and slipstitch opening closed. Press carefully.

3. Make two pillows 2¼″ × 2″, following Group A directions on page 15, using white crepe—except, be-

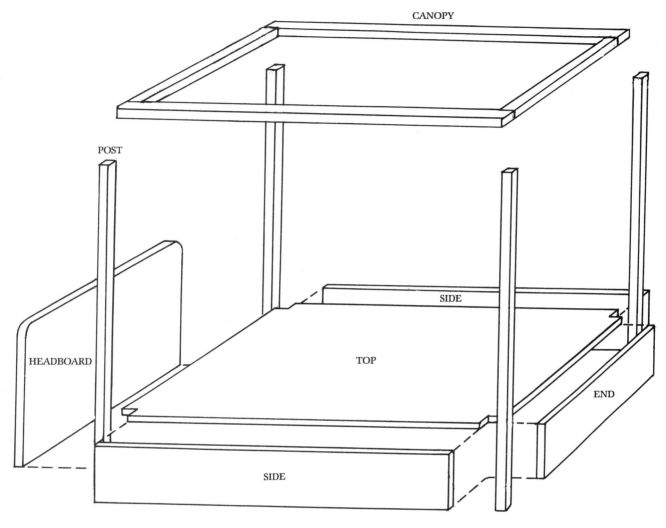

Figure 42

fore stitching pillow pieces together, trim pillow front with floral print fabric same as for bedspread, placing outer edge of trim ½″ from raw edge of fabric, as shown in *Figure 43*.

Figure 43

CURTAINS

1. Make curtains following directions on page 17, using floral print fabric.

2. For curtain rods, see page 9.

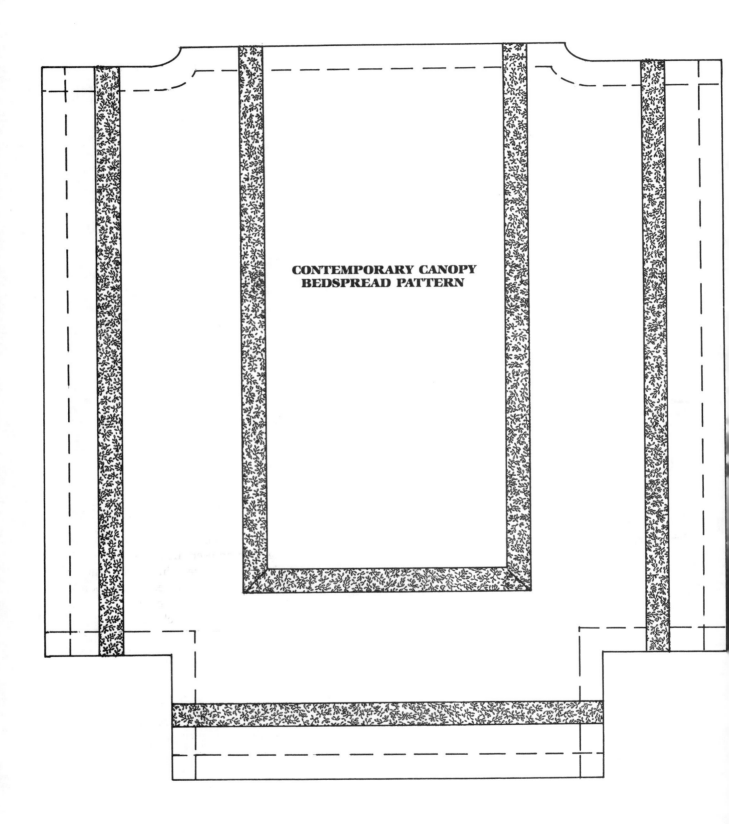

CONTEMPORARY CANOPY
BEDSPREAD PATTERN

CHAPTER 5

Miniature Accessories

Accessories will turn a house into a home. Pictures from a favorite place, a great-aunt's quilt and a placemat lovingly embroidered by a close friend are just a few items that make my own home special. This chapter shows how to make some accessories that will add warmth and a comfortable feeling to the room settings in this book. Collect ideas, then experiment with some of your own.

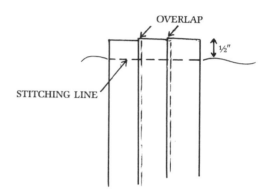

Figure 44

about 2″, secure braided end in a closed drawer and continue braiding with an even, medium tension.

3. When braiding is complete, wind loosely into an oval shape, keeping braid flat; tuck ends to back and slip-stitch rounds together as you wind; see *Figure 45*.

4. When rug is complete, stitch across ends of braiding strips to secure. Tuck loose ends to back of rug, and stitch in place. Press rug with a warm iron.

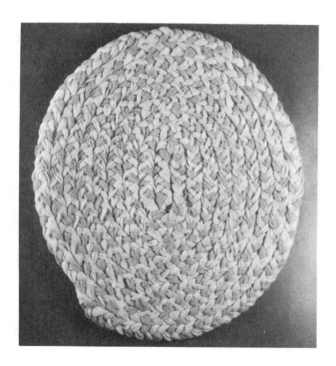

BRAIDED RUG

Shown in color on the inside front cover

Size: 4″ × 4¾″ oval.

Materials and Equipment: Twill tape ¼″ wide, three packages (about 12 yards total), in desired colors. Thread. Sewing machine. Sewing needle. Scissors. Ruler. Iron.

Directions: Refer to *Figures 44–45* for assembly.

1. Secure the three ends of the different packages of tape together by overlapping them slightly and stitching ½″ from edge, as shown in *Figure 44*.

2. Braid strips with right sides facing you; after

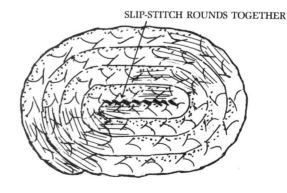

Figure 45

BREAKFAST TRAY

Shown in color on the inside back cover

Size: 1¼″ × 3⅛″ × 1″ high.

Materials and Equipment: Read *Equipment* and *Materials* sections in Chapter 1 for basic supplies. Scraps of ⅛″ balsa wood. 16 round wooden toothpicks, pointed at both ends. Scraps of ⅛″-square balsa-wood strips. White spray paint. Clear varnish or polyurethane. Glue. X-ACTO knife. Ruler. Small nail and tack hammer. Tracing paper.

Directions: Refer to *Figures 46–47* for assembly.

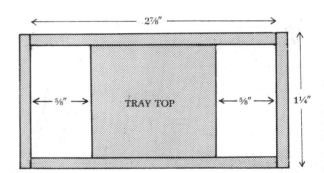

Figure 46

BREAKFAST TRAY BOTTOM PATTERN

1. Trace pattern for tray bottom and use to cut two pieces from balsa wood; mark dots on each piece following pattern. From balsa wood, cut one 1″ × 1¾″ tray top. From balsa strips, cut two pieces 2⅞″ long and two pieces 1¼″ long. Cut toothpicks in half, then trim cut edges so each toothpick piece is ⅞″ long; each piece will have one pointed end.

2. Carefully tap 16 tiny starter holes around each tray bottom piece with a tack hammer and small nail following the marked dots. Insert and glue points of toothpicks into holes, keeping them in even vertical lines; let dry.

3. On a flat surface, arrange and glue balsa strips and tray top together as shown in *Figure 46*; let dry.

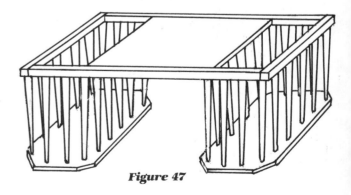

Figure 47

4. Carefully glue top and bottom together as shown in *Figure 47*; let dry.

5. Spray entire tray with white paint, using two or three coats if necessary, and letting paint dry between coats. When final coat is dry, finish with clear varnish or polyurethane and let dry.

EMBROIDERED PLACEMAT AND NAPKIN

Shown in color on the inside back cover

Size: *Mat:* 1¼″ × 1¾″. *Napkin:* ⅝″ × 1″, folded.
Materials and Equipment: Scrap of fine white linen. Thread. Embroidery floss, one strand each lavender, gray and green. Sewing machine. Sewing and embroidery needles. Ruler. Iron. Pencil. Glue. Double-faced tape.
Directions: Refer to *Figures 48–49* for assembly.

1. Cut two 1¾″ × 2¼″ pieces of linen for mat and one 1¼″ × 1½″ piece for napkin.

2. With pencil, mark off a 1″ × 1¼″ rectangle, centered on right side of napkin. Embroider flower in lower left-hand corner, inside marked rectangle, following *Figure 48* and stitch details; work flower in lavender, stem in gray and leaves in green. Fold edges of napkin ⅛″ to wrong side; glue to secure.

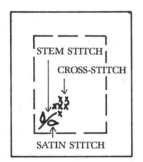

Figure 48

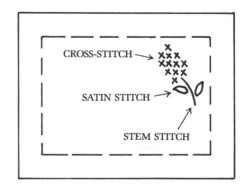

Figure 49

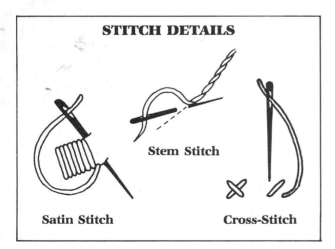

3. With pencil, mark off a 1¼″ × 1¾″ rectangle, centered on right side of one placemat piece. Embroider flower in upper right hand corner, inside marked rectangle, following *Figure 49* and stitch details; work flower in lavender, stem in gray and leaves in green. Stitch linen pieces together with right sides facing, making ¼″ seams; leave an opening in one side for turning. Turn mat to right side and slip-stitch opening closed. Press carefully.

4. Fold napkin in half, and use double-faced tape to secure it to left side of mat. Use tape or mini-hold to attach mat to breakfast tray, or make a set of mats to use in a kitchen or dining room.

QUILT STAND

Shown in color on the inside back cover

Size: 3″ × 1¼″ × 2¾″ high.

Materials and Equipment: Read *Equipment* and *Materials* sections in Chapter 1 for basic supplies. Scraps of ³⁄₁₆″ balsa wood. Wooden dowel, ⅛″ diameter. Glue. Wood stain. X-ACTO knife. Ruler. Pencil. Small nail. Tracing paper.

Directions: Refer to *Figure 50* for assembly.

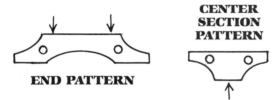

END PATTERN

CENTER SECTION PATTERN

1. Trace pattern for end and use to cut four pieces from ³⁄₁₆″ balsa wood; mark dots on one side of each piece following pattern. Trace pattern for center section and use to cut two pieces from ³⁄₁₆″ balsa wood; mark dots on both sides of each piece following pattern. From dowel, cut the following lengths: four 2¾″, eight 1″ and one 2½″.

2. Stain all pieces as desired and let dry thoroughly.

3. Carefully make very shallow starter holes for dowels using small nail as follows:

    A. Make two holes on one *side* of each end piece in marked positions; make two holes along one *edge* of each in positions indicated by arrows.

    B. Make two holes on *both sides* of each center section in marked positions; make one hole along one *edge* of each in position indicated by arrow.

4. Following *Figure 50*, glue dowels to end and center section pieces, fitting dowels carefully into starter holes as follows:

    A. Glue 2¾″ dowels between end pieces.

    B. Glue 2½″ dowel between center section pieces.

    C. Glue 1″ dowels between ends and center section pieces as shown; let dry thoroughly, standing the piece upright and adjusting so all angles are straight.

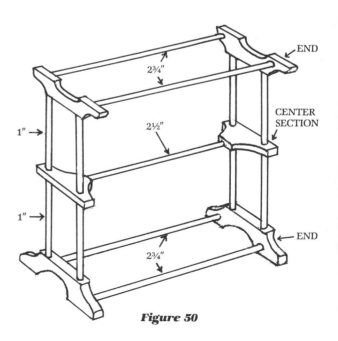

Figure 50

PATCHWORK QUILT

Shown in color on the inside back cover

Size: 2⅜″ × 4¼″.

Materials and Equipment: Read *Equipment* and *Materials* sections in Chapter 2 for basic supplies. Scraps of lightweight cotton in assorted prints. Thin batting. Thread. Sewing needle. Scissors. Ruler. Pencil. Pins. Iron.

Directions: Refer to *Figure 51* for assembly.

1. From assorted fabrics, cut fifty ⅝″-square pieces for patchwork top. Cut one 3⅛″ × 5″ piece for backing from one of the assorted fabrics. Cut one 2⅜″ × 4¼″ piece of batting.

2. With right sides facing and raw edges even, stitch squares together ⅛″ from edges, making five rows with ten squares in each row. Press all seams to one side (toward the darker fabric).

3. With right sides facing and raw edges even, stitch rows together matching seams carefully and making ⅛″ seams; piece will measure 2⅛″ × 4″. Press all seams to one side.

4. Press all raw edges of backing ⅛″ to wrong side. Center batting on wrong side of backing; pin and baste in place. Center patchwork, right side up, over batting; pin and baste in place. See *Figure 51*.

5. To create border, fold pressed edges of backing ¼″ toward patchwork top, mitering corners; pin in place. Slip-stitch border to patchwork invisibly.

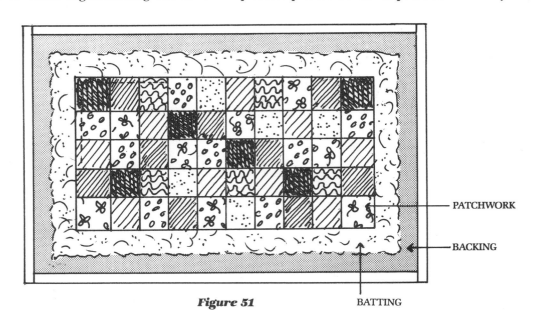

PATCHWORK

BACKING

Figure 51   BATTING

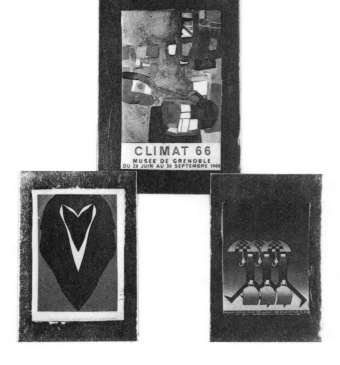

LAMPSHADE COVER

Shown in color on the inside back cover

Directions:

1. Cut a strip of fabric ½″ more than height and double the widest circumference of your lampshade.

2. Turn both long edges of fabric strip ½″ to the wrong side and press. With right sides facing, stitch the short ends together ¼″ from edges.

3. Make a small running stitch by hand along both edges of fabric ⅛″ from folded edge, using doubled thread and leaving ends of thread long for tying.

4. Place fabric cover, right side out, over lampshade and pull thread ends to gather top and bottom edges so they hug the lampshade snugly. Once gathers are even, tie the thread ends and conceal them on the inside.

POSTERS

Materials and Equipment: Foil-backed poster board *or* any stiff paper, such as oaktag, and aluminum foil. Pictures from magazines or catalogs, stamps, scraps of fabric or wallpaper, etc. Scissors. Glue. X-ACTO knife. Mini-hold or double-faced tape.

Directions:

1. Cut boards to desired sizes for posters (½″ larger all around than the pictures you are featuring). If using aluminum foil and stiff paper, glue foil smoothly to one side of paper, then cut to size.

2. Glue pictures, stamps, fabric, wallpaper, etc., to foil side of board, centered so that the foil frames the picture.

3. Use mini-hold or double-faced tape to attach posters to wall.

METRIC CONVERSION CHART

CONVERTING INCHES TO CENTIMETERS AND YARDS TO METERS

mm — millimeters   cm — centimeters   m — meters

INCHES INTO MILLIMETERS AND CENTIMETERS
(Slightly rounded off for convenience)

inches	mm		cm	inches	cm	inches	cm	inches	cm
⅛	3mm			5	12.5	21	53.5	38	96.5
¼	6mm			5½	14	22	56	39	99
⅜	10mm	or	1cm	6	15	23	58.5	40	101.5
½	13mm	or	1.3cm	7	18	24	61	41	104
⅝	15mm	or	1.5cm	8	20.5	25	63.5	42	106.5
¾	20mm	or	2cm	9	23	26	66	43	109
⅞	22mm	or	2.2cm	10	25.5	27	68.5	44	112
1	25mm	or	2.5cm	11	28	28	71	45	114.5
1¼	32mm	or	3.2cm	12	30.5	29	73.5	46	117
1½	38mm	or	3.8cm	13	33	30	76	47	119.5
1¾	45mm	or	4.5cm	14	35.5	31	79	48	122
2	50mm	or	5cm	15	38	32	81.5	49	124.5
2½	65mm	or	6.5cm	16	40.5	33	84	50	127
3	75mm	or	7.5cm	17	43	34	86.5		
3½	90mm	or	9cm	18	46	35	89		
4	100mm	or	10cm	19	48.5	36	91.5		
4½	115mm	or	11.5cm	20	51	37	94		

YARDS TO METERS
(Slightly rounded off for convenience)

yards	meters	yards	meters	yards	meters	yards	meters	yards	meters
⅛	0.15	2⅛	1.95	4⅛	3.80	6⅛	5.60	8⅛	7.45
¼	0.25	2¼	2.10	4¼	3.90	6¼	5.75	8¼	7.55
⅜	0.35	2⅜	2.20	4⅜	4.00	6⅜	5.85	8⅜	7.70
½	0.50	2½	2.30	4½	4.15	6½	5.95	8½	7.80
⅝	0.60	2⅝	2.40	4⅝	4.25	6⅝	6.10	8⅝	7.90
¾	0.70	2¾	2.55	4¾	4.35	6¾	6.20	8¾	8.00
⅞	0.80	2⅞	2.65	4⅞	4.50	6⅞	6.30	8⅞	8.15
1	0.95	3	2.75	5	4.60	7	6.40	9	8.25
1⅛	1.05	3⅛	2.90	5⅛	4.70	7⅛	6.55	9⅛	8.35
1¼	1.15	3¼	3.00	5¼	4.80	7¼	6.65	9¼	8.50
1⅜	1.30	3⅜	3.10	5⅜	4.95	7⅜	6.75	9⅜	8.60
1½	1.40	3½	3.20	5½	5.05	7½	6.90	9½	8.70
1⅝	1.50	3⅝	3.35	5⅝	5.15	7⅝	7.00	9⅝	8.80
1¾	1.60	3¾	3.45	5¾	5.30	7¾	7.10	9¾	8.95
1⅞	1.75	3⅞	3.55	5⅞	5.40	7⅞	7.20	9⅞	9.05
2	1.85	4	3.70	6	5.50	8	7.35	10	9.15

AVAILABLE FABRIC WIDTHS

25"	65cm	50"	127cm
27"	70cm	54"/56"	140cm
35"/36"	90cm	58"/60"	150cm
39"	100cm	68"/70"	175cm
44"/45"	115cm	72"	180cm
48"	122cm		

AVAILABLE ZIPPER LENGTHS

4"	10cm	10"	25cm	22"	55cm
5"	12cm	12"	30cm	24"	60cm
6"	15cm	14"	35cm	26"	65cm
7"	18cm	16"	40cm	28"	70cm
8"	20cm	18"	45cm	30"	75cm
9"	22cm	20"	50cm		